a scrap of linen, a bone

a scrap of linen, a bone

Poems

Ginger Murchison

Press 53
Winston-Salem

Press 53, LLC
PO Box 30314
Winston-Salem, NC 27130

First Edition

A TOM LOMBARDO POETRY SELECTION

Cover design and layout by Kevin Morgan Watson

Cover art, "Roots and Leaf, 1," Copyright © 2015 by Dawn D. Surratt
instagram.com/ddhanna

Author photo by Wm. J. Mynatt

Printed on acid-free paper
ISBN 978-1-941209-33-2

for Thomas Lux

Acknowledgments

Grateful acknowledgment is made to the editors of the following publications in which these poems first appeared:

Atlanta Review: "The Saindon Family Mouth," "Small Craft Advisory"

Chattahoochee Review: "A Substitute for Talking," "From the Deck in Mid-November," under a slightly different title.

Terminus Magazine: "Abacus," "The Insult"

Horticulture: "Thrift"

Poetry Kanto: "The Pear Tree," "Whitman's Hermit Thrush," "The Wind," "On Stone Mountain"

Connotations: "April," "A walk on the Beach," "Discards," "Mandatory Evacuation"

MEAD: The Magazine of Literature and Libations: "Connemara," "The Failure of Archaeology," "April"

"Something Back to the Birds," under a slightly different title, appeared in the anthology, *Best of Toadlily Press: New and Selected, 2011*, edited by Myrna Goodman and Meredith Trede, 2011

"Small Craft Advisory" appeared in *The Gift of Experience: 10ᵗʰ Anniversary Anthology*, edited by Daniel Veach, 2005

"Lesson with Flashcards" appeared in the anthology *Java Monkey Speaks III*, edited by Kodac Harrison and Collin Kelley, 2010

"Vocabulary" appeared in the anthology *Shout Them from the Mountain Tops: Georgia Poems*, (Georgia Council of Teachers of English, 2004)

"The Orchid" and "Every Last Time" appeared in *Southern Poetry Anthology*, (Texas Review Press, 2008)

Contents

Introduction by Thomas Lux   xi

i

Failure of Archaeology	3
On Stone Mountain	4
The Saindon Family Mouth	5
Vocabulary	6
Gravedigger	7
Mid-Western Madonna	8
The pear tree	9
Leaf fall	10
The Fish Houses	11
Out here	12
April	13
River	14
Small Craft Advisory	15
The Insult	16
A Walk on the Beach	17
"When the heart dies, it dies entire"	18

ii

Wartime Measures	21
Hardwood Floors	22
Lines and Squares	23
Mandatory Evacuation	24
The wind	25
Acorns	26
Evening	27
Honor System	28
Every Last Time	29
Thrift	30
A Good Time to Die	31

The Orchid   32
Birdsong   33
Whitman's Hermit Thrush   34
Asylum   35
At the Holy Well of Tobernalt   36
Gravity   37

iii

Roller Coaster   41
Lesson with Flashcards   42
Something Back to the Birds   43
Not Quite Ever After   44
The East Berliner, 1989   45
From the Chicago Train   46
Abacus   47
That First Leaving   48
Violin   49
Shambala   50
From the Deck in Mid-November   51
A Substitute for Talking   52
Discards   53
For the two of you   54
I don't know yet   55
Connemara   56
Delta to West Palm   57

Notes   59
In Gratitude   65
Author biography   67
Cover artist biography   69

Introduction

What struck me first about this book was its sly sense of humor; not easy humor, not lazy humor, but a kind of joyful wryness, an attitude found only in adults who've taken some knocks and are still standing.

One of my favorite poems is "The Saindon Family Mouth." It starts with a photo of thirteen family members lined up beside a '30's Ford. She calls them a "breadline" (therefore no need to mention The Great Depression) and writes that there was "not an upper lip to be seen." And "they were a choir with its mouth shut, not one smile, / as if the smile hadn't yet evolved." The poem is a loving portrait of a strong family in hard times, and its humor and playful-ness lifts each of the thirteen to a realm of unique dignity.

Birds show up (thankfully) with some regularity in these poems. "Something Back to the Birds" begins with a wonderful image of a child building a birdhouse with his father: the boy stands on a chair so his hammer-swings are at the same level as those of his father. The lines, of course, which I'm slightly paraphrasing, are a metaphor for father/son relationships. I'd never read a simpler image on the subject that felt more authentic. Birds are, after all, "holes in the sky through which we can see God." That quote is not in the poem, but the boy in the poem, I think, would agree with it.

It's hard to write good poems about our own children: we're too close to them. Ginger Murchison's beats the odds on this dilemma. The above poem makes this clear, particularly when you read the detail that the boy also kills a long snake "inching toward the bluebird eggs."

In a poem about her daughter, whom she comes upon trying to teach her dog to read with flashcards, Murchison writes: "I know I'm as close as I'll ever get / to how grass feels in the rain." There's another poem in which she pushes her daughter in a swing. She notices her daughter's pure child-joy "reaching for the pull / she felt in the curve that wanted her back." We've all pushed a child in a swing. After reading this poem, I will take a little more pleasure in it the next time I do.

I hear the bones of the Midwest in these poems' speech rhythms. I also hear some Southern cadences and at least a decade of Texas in the music of Murchison's voice.

These are *made* poems. These are *earned* poems. These are poems of a full-fledged grownup who understands and celebrates the "slow hungers" that "breathe / beneath leveled dreams, / the South's muscular sky / painted over now, paler blue." This book will offer you welcome and pleasure.

—Thomas Lux

i

The Failure of Archaeology

After the ashes have cooled,
the taste of catastrophe gone
from every mouth, the scholars
will, inch by inch
            dig down
to a bracelet, a scrap
of linen, a bone and write
the story without us—
            no one left
to remember the sea-grass smell
wafting in on the breeze
the river-damp rusting
wrought iron—
            no one left
to say what really burned there,
what words drifted
       on salt air,
            forgotten

now that the flames have died.

On Stone Mountain

Back toward the time when
the world, without footprints, broke open
to the scraggles of leaf and limb with barely
a foothold in hairline cracks in the bald, gray stone,

we came with our lunches—Jason, just a boy,
and me, already the age of labored breathing—
to rehearse state capitals, remember Huck, and hide
crusts for whatever hunkered down waiting for dark.

Like grave robbers at the crypts of pharaohs,
we stared into pools the color of soot, worlds
mired in a different time, the fairy shrimp, ghosts
in chiffon, white as fear, life, sure enough, still

pushing out of pre-history, waiting to crawl
out of their tiny seas, nature intent, maybe,
on moving ahead without us, or back. Maybe
the world once looked just like this. Would again.

The Saindon Family Mouth

Thirteen of them (my mother ninth)
in one of those Depression photos, a breadline
beside a nineteen-thirty-something Ford,
the one up front, one foot up,
Clyde Barrow style, on the running board
not an upper lip to be seen.
Nothing there to stud, or pierce, or gloss. Not one lip
of consequence to purse or curl with recklessness. Not one
of them ever paid to smoke a cigarette or model Revlon,
they were a choir with its mouth shut, not one smile,
as if the smile hadn't yet evolved.

We grew up believing that straight and narrow lip
meant austerity—as if some John Wayne grain of grit
had worked its way into our lineage, a line,
Churchillian, drawn in the sand that stopped us without a word,
that razor lip, starched as rhetoric, a wire
across the road like the fine line we walked
toward that arrow-straight horizon
that was neither Earth nor space,
and—the last word already said—promised nothing.

Vocabulary

The first thing I remember seeing dead
was my grandfather, lying there
as if a prairie wind had blown him down,
skin taut on long and angled bone,
his face, plains dust, lips cracked by cold,
his Sunday shirt starched stiff, a contradiction
to his hands—fingers, dried
cornstalks in August,
folded in unfamiliar ease.

They came by ones, as if there'd been an ad—
an opportunity to see a neighbor sleeping
in his dining room. Carved faces
looked at him, then at the wall,
the flowers there dead-brown as he was.

Pretending immortality, sons in suspenders
on the back porch squinted at cigarettes
smoked too far down and pulled at ties
like boys caught telling lies.
Homemade bread rose in the kitchen
to choruses of *Inka Dinka Do*
and *Won't You Come Home, Bill Bailey*,
my own mother louder than the rest.
Even the priest who bowed his head
beside the body grabbed a beer,
pressed its cold against his face, sang, too.

I couldn't tell where death began and ended,
but that whole farmhouse tilted toward the casket
with the weight of my new word.

Gravedigger

for my grandfather 1896-1962

A chunk of tobacco deep in his cheek and smelling
of dirt that never gave up its grip,
he started work in the dark, broke open the ground
to spend most of his day in a hole,
shovel after shovelful over his shoulder—so much
to dig up to dig down—
shouldering his way to the bottom of every grave,
his shirt black-wet either with sweat
or the slow rain crusting the dirty snow, every day
digging down to a place just like this—
another hole in another pewter-gray day, this time,
just the three of us looking down,
nothing to give back but a handful of earth.

Mid-Western Madonna

Against Kansas dust the color of struggle,
street kids, stray dogs and flies
compete for scraps of yesterday's waste
in the back-alley brick-oven heat.

Little more than a child herself,
on a three-legged stool, barefoot,
belly-soft with new birth, her flimsy skirt
wadded between her legs, she is all but lost

in the half-shade of a half-choked-to-death
spindly tree, slapping lard-slick dough
at the side of her naked thigh,
her infant daughter at her breast,

an ageless ache.
Not much to suckle there
but the knowledge of breast and thigh.
All it will ever pay her to know.

The pear tree

that for years
flowered has fallen
home to the borers

their greed
for not only the fruit
but the flesh of the tree

hard to say
what we look like to them
worming our way through these rooms

our hungers fatal, too

Leaf fall

piles up   at the porch steps
    withers into compost and ash
the whole world   going brown
    but I keep sweeping up   deny
all these deaths   buy
  flowering plants   go on
    eating and sleeping   pretend
 we weren't   born for this too
  our bodies   designed for storms
the shock   of every rude thing
  the births behind us   obsessions
    liquor and worry and famine
even for what   we've forgotten
     we'd die for
  yellowed flesh   wizened
    with age spots   and wrinkled
failures just creases around our eyes
    bellies sponge   thighs
  too weak for stairs even for the love
we can't live without   whoever
  we've been   or might become
buried   inside shapes
    we used to despise

The Fish Houses

Like seeds cracked open, blooming in the ooze of fish and mud
the blast of rain and hurricanes, they're the story of wet boots, wet nets,
wet nights, outlasting the fishermen who smoked, drank, cursed and slept there—
their metal roofs stars in a galaxy turned upside-down, burning
its slow way to collapse, wordless as an offshore fog, a patience
in the wind's rushed syllables coming forth and forth.

A century of sun-ups, birds and storms, and they're still here
knee-deep in Pine Island Sound like old women wading a puddle, skirts up
to keep their hems dry—grandmothers battered by history, their flesh
gone slack under Sunday bonnets worn too many seasons
and stories they'll die with.

Out here

the air beside me remembers your place,
each day rich with the river-grass moldering,
evenings sodden with sins,
minimal, monumental mistakes.

Out here, the shadows, greedy as pimps,
spread over roof tops, want everything,
but headwaters can't help thinking *south*.
The thinnest root, because of a light
it won't ever see and can't name,
goes on steaming under the piled-up snow.
Even the wind, always sweeping up,
tries to look busy in the next stand of pines.

April

and the cottonwoods would lose their minds

        let go

their fluff-wrapped seeds—our window open
to the whistle and rattle of leaves
till every last seed

        took its spin

on the wind, straining for the shoreline silt
of the river in our back yard where we'd

        watch them float

delicate as a bride's nightgown
and later, when the river

        overswelled its banks

we'd stay up all night sandbagging
another whole year's seedlings lost

River

Late afternoons, we'd tuck up our hems
under Minisa Bridge, scrape our white knees
on scrub brush and drowned trees to slide

down the dirt bank past milk-weed
gone to seed, cattails and trash to sit on stones
at the edge of the river and giggle and smoke,

waiting to wolf-whistle North High's rowing team.
In the shadows where the milk-chocolate river
unfolded, ooze between our toes, we'd strip,

risk long-legged insects, leeches and mothers
for the silt slick on our thighs, the air thick
with the smell of honeysuckle, mud—the rest

of the day somewhere downstream. We didn't
know why, but none of us wanted
to go home to polite kitchens and mothers

patiently waiting for what happened next,
the way women have always waited for hunter husbands,
kept vigils and prayed at the entrance of mines.

Small Craft Advisory

to my son Jason

It takes serendipitous, found things to make a raft,
some nailed-together boards, maybe an old wooden door.

You'll need a steering oar, but mostly trust
the raft to find a current, dangle your feet, and drift

where drifting never is a dirty word. Those holes
where the water's thick are mink and muskrat homes.

If you're quick, you'll see a snake slice the brackish water
for a meal of frog or fish or salamander. Lie face up.

Imagine you're another Galileo. What he learned,
counting with his heartbeat, set him on the path to prove,

you know, the sun the center of the universe,
but he couldn't say so. Stubborn men make stubborn laws.

Take some water, bread and honey,
apples, too, and, especially, a friend.

It will take both of you to untie the language
and discover the insignificance of speech.

The Insult

Check out the retard
doesn't sound like an insult
to my daughter. She doesn't know
the boy behind us in the food court
loves his joke, loves even more
that he's worked it for a laugh.

I want to slap him,
say a thing so wide, I'd drive
spikes of guilt inside his spine,
wish him a world of flower stems
chopped off where the blooms begin,
salmon plunging belly-up, downstream,

but I'd rather he just look at her.
She isn't in his word,
and he will need her
if he ever wants to know
how far the sky goes
or how to stay close to the ground.

A Walk on the Beach

A beach accumulates the sea's debris:
    washed-up bone, shell, salt-dried, eyeless sea-life.
        That's understandable. But this is flesh,

the indignity of bloat, blue
    in a purple swimsuit, heart-stopped
        and drowned, the ungodly truth of him

dragged here, the curious drawn in,
    the way a street musician's violin
        is desolate enough to throw a quarter at,

and this little bit of breeze, the waves,
    their forth and back, not even noticing
        his wife and daughters holding each other up

in some other language, already left
    with the job of pushing the rest of this day
        into what they know is called tomorrow.

I pull my son close, tell him to turn his music down,
    grab my daughter's hand—touch
        how I know what still belongs to me.

"When the heart dies, it dies entire"

after Kurt Brown

Mars understood that something enormous bred into him made him run
danger in good genes that   looking for a way out   uncoils
tears out ahead of the will   for the two minutes   along the rail
start to finish   but not this   not this bursting heart   not
the track's falling away beneath his hooves   not how he'll go wrong
tear off   crash into the far rail   his rider over it   crumple
like a ruined city   everything known unknown in a stone-heart dark

Heart matters in a racehorse   Given out   it's a snapped cable
all the wires down   that hunger to finish   gone
like a spoken prayer   *Mars*   the announcer says   *is taking no part*
as if Mars   were a spoiled child   pouting over a plate of asparagus

The five million went to Gentildonna   the sun went on its own track
the Mike de Koch crew   packed up   for the trip back
& the fans ripped up their tickets on number 2 & cursed their rotten luck

ii

Wartime Measures

They meant something safe,
all those Mason jars
labeled and lined up like soldiers
on shelves in the cellar—
every jewel color of summer preserved
with rationed sugar my mother,
half-afraid, hoarded and hid
in the hollow base of our kitchen table.
She was new to war, all ninety pounds
of her, head-to-foot berry-stained,
bent to the purple boil
in the weekend-sweet kitchen heat.

Weekdays, she donned coveralls,
rode the bus an hour each way
to work the night shift
in Boeing's assembly plant.
We did our part, my sister and I—
wagonloads of scrap metal meant
munitions, dimes added up
to savings bonds. We didn't know
where the metal and money went,
but we were part of the cause—
my thumbprint in the paraffin
cooling to solid under the shiny lids—
all those star-spangled jars
in formation in the patriotic dark
like the beads of rosaries we fingered.

Hardwood Floors

Night after night that whole summer
he'd saw the oak strips, nudge them

snug side by side, test them for level,
then satisfied with the fit, the grain

and color, nail each one home,
he and the house all dust.

While the rest of us shifted corner to corner
with the china and chests of drawers,

Dad and that wood—all sawdust
and sweat—made their way wall to wall.

I crawled beside him—wanted
in on the prayer—wanted that floor

planed, sanded and varnished—
its shine whatever he had in mind.

Lines and Squares

for my sister, master quilter

We learned to pay attention to lines—
line up block letters, careful
to cut on them, color within them,
stand in them and walk the fine ones.
Kansas summers we played hopscotch,
chalked squares on the sidewalk, tossed stones
toward a place called *safe*, a place
where we'd turn around and come back.
Any rain and the lines would disappear.

Saturdays, our quarters in knotted squares
in our shoes, we'd race downtown
for the Orpheum at First & Main,
risk fiery Hell on lies to get in for a dime, watch
the caped avenger save the heroine, the planet
the universe week after week—*to be continued*
all we could predict.

Invisible lines kept us
on our separate sides of the bed, the backseat
of the Ford, a territorial squaring off—
what was hers was hers, mine was mine
—practice for the moving apart
we would one day do, for that time
when this line, too, would disappear—

just lines and squares, yellowed
in trunks somewhere. Buried too.

Mandatory Evacuation

and the blunt face of the storm
the wheat grass   raking the sand
and the worn-thin sky   so bruised
the sun can't get through
and the storm smell
and the day   tasting like dust and metal
even then   they won't go
then everything   nailed to the wall
of fear   everything
they've put down money for
even the light   changed forever
piers   matchsticks
out of the water
trees   piled up Tinker Toys   roofs
paper airplanes   households
split wide   like a lightning-strike sky
blown-wet curtains flapping
where a wall had been
and even with the waves quiet again
anything living   lives on some mercy   none
of the reasons for staying remembered
all around drowned
what's gone
keeping on being gone
and the birds   complaining
                              in the sore air

The wind

has laid the day's
yellow dust
on the window sills
and the river

thunder
riding the same air
as Paganini

Acorns

Weeks now and acorns still pound
the roof, the skylights, the wooden decks.
Maybe that oak, covering as it does the whole house,
has to let go some of the nurturing, stir
somehow beyond itself—every odd year
dropping these gifts we lack inspiration
to know how to use—blessings to scatter
like our efforts to paint, play the cello, or dance.

You can't help but admire the pummeling
insistence, keeping it up. That well.
That long. With that attitude.
No swerving off the path, no stopping
to consider at crossroads, no legal pad out
any midnight to line up the pros and cons.
No flying off in search of some truth
or hunkering down in a protest.
Just every day's bearing down to keep it up
at a height we have to look up to.

Evening

At this angle of hours,
the orchestra all oboes—
blown goodbyes
through the sea oats—

the windfall pears
have mostly gone to ooze
seeped into the earth,
all these trees
unclothed to cold,
the last of the shining
downstream by now.

Slow hungers breathe
beneath leveled dreams,
the South's muscular sky
painted over now, paler blue.

Honor System

The August we were married, we didn't need the bridge,
walked the bone-dry bottom of the Arkansas, weeds
and trash where you'd expect an underwater catfish flash.

My dad's old friend, skin dry as the hot-sand bottom
of that river, remembered every Kansas dry spell, told
how every country store had books thick with accounts

the farmers couldn't pay till the last crop came in, how,
what with irrigation and the Colorado farmers taking
what they needed, that river would be dried to a trickle

before it got to Kansas, how it wasn't likely he would ever
see it full again, how just last year, though, that one patch
up against the house he'd asked God to bless stayed green,

made a wagonload of sweet potatoes he sold off the table
honor system, how farming is dirty work, and even that
is coming to a close, how on the way to town, now, he'll forget

all about that four-way stop, how a good amount of rain
and he'll have purple peas and butterbeans for that table,
but whatever's out there will be gone by noon.

Every Last Time

everything about the South boiling over
    like another consequence
        in the heaving night air
pungent with mildewed magnolia blossoms
    ripened to rotting, dank end
        of the blooming season
cattails like damnation's fingers, moss trailing
    its tangling like uncombed beards
        of father confessors
and live oaks, bent like arthritic ancestors
    overhanging oppression
        each leaf a dry-thirsting
for secrets to whisper along limb to limb
    the hissing song, those long sighs
        of night-drawling bird calls
and me, each breath splintered and even today
    turning still, every last time
        into the wrong ending

Thrift

Dad always looked like God at creation,
      on his knees, bent, coaxing some scraggle
           or other with hands he'd earned in the dirt,

some root wanting other weather, dreaming
      its feet wet in streambeds or the yellow rot
           of a hothouse. Not one thing in our yard

was meant to grow there, but maybe like us,
      believed in miracles, one more chance
           to measure up. I never knew their names.

From last year's vacation photos a blur
      of blossoms strewn on the sea-cliff's blown stone—
           all summer's *ameria maritime,*

cleft-clinging paper-thin pinks and stark whites—
      Thrift, in only a few grains of dust
           and, maybe from him, how to live on a prayer.

A Good Time to Die

Another snow out his fifth-floor window,
our small group looks down into white sheets—
just like he wants it.
A good time to die.

Fists in knots,
he tries to will winter into his veins.
And why not? He's made our lives with his hands
all out of nothing—beat the cold, the system,
the odds—won by a mile, by inches,
sometimes a hair. Everything but this.
When the morphine hits, he drops,
a pebble in snow,
deeper into the sheets.

Over vending-machine coffee and small talk,
our thin laugh pretends it's any old day.

The Orchid

I fill the house and all the porches with flowers,
orchids mostly.

They are what art in the dark wants to become.
One—the purple Crayola calls 39-A—

its long, naked stalk done finally with flowering,
I toss into the compost. Weeks later,

audacity stirs, flings four purple blooms
out of that rot—a ferocious eloquence

I bring back in the house. It isn't breeding;
a simple potato will do the same thing,

hard-wired as it is to go on to a future
it can't imagine or name, like what's blossoming

in my sister's lungs, another hard winter coming.

Birdsong

when did we stop listening
you there   me here
and summer already this far gone

Whitman's Hermit Thrush

The brightest star down, this gray-brown meager bird's
        sweet, reedy mourning is one brittle pitch

grief large enough for the pain, an orange wire
        right through the brain, a bullet to bite

one piece of clean, cold metal scraping another
        like hunger, a train with its brakes on

one clear note of song on and on
        the screech of a screen door—

    somebody leaving
               someone come home

Asylum

for the mental patients and the hundreds of unopened suitcases found
after New York's Willard State Hospital for the Insane closed in 1995

Like orphans with suitcases, the gravely mute are dropped
at the dead end of state care—each one a name in pica type

beside words like *irrational, confused*—even this place of promise,
where time moves like a land mass, smells of urine and fright.

Here, men are measured in cc's and grams. Innocence walks on the verge
of an open grave looking down at a sick yellow light in the dust,

light laid down in a cockeyed pattern, the grain of Venetian-blind slats
a labyrinth that will swallow it, an insistent hum the numb oblivion

of naked light bulbs, where it will pay to learn to be dead,
where the living stand over the dead to make sure they stay dead.

No one needs unpack a suitcase here. No one needs remember the houses
they were born to or the idea of spring in a print dress. No one needs

an old Valentine, a draft card, or photos of friends in dress shoes
and hats on holiday. No one here needs the fire gone out in their hearts.

At the Holy Well of Tobernalt

Like one of those shawled women
bent over beads any weather
in the world's empty churches,
she's come with her Down Syndrome son,
her shoes like faith handed down,
her coat probably as old as he is,
twenty, maybe twenty-five,
and her shoulders shaped
by what it's taken to believe
for both of them.

His name, he says, is Evan,
his hands, knots in his jacket pockets
as if Evan were a stone hidden there
for making wishes. He's set loose leaves
and sticks on the water like little boats.
Thursdays, he smiles, *is Tobernalt,*
the one thing besides his mother
he's sure of, that this water
will be here next Thursday,
that it will carry whatever it's given to carry.

Gravity

between the corset and the right to vote
while Grover Cleveland and the cocksure rich
moved the railroad, the presses
even by God
that bothersome river,
Annie Edson Taylor in her best hat
serious morning light on that water
threw herself into the God-fearing mid-air
over the falls at Niagara
                        for money

and the flesh had been warned
about a fall
            that pride goeth
            money's the root
not to mention all that talk
about a woman's place
and Freud ready
with his theory about women
                and

                        relinquished

                                    equilibrium

and still even now
all these thinner survivals
the flesh not ever done
                with desiring

Roller Coaster

It starts with the climbing in,
nerved-up enough
for that defiance
of gravity, the slow-grind
rackety-clack one-inch cog
at a time—the mystery of machinery,
the sane and safe weightedness
of stiff-starched values,
wondering if there were
sins we'd committed
since our last confession, then
at the top, out on the edge,
beyond the solid-ground world
parents live in, test life,
theirs and our own, up where
we are a hole in the sky,
wholly abandoned in the eyes-
shut, heart-stopped drop,
like lawlessness on falling's
crisp speed, the first curve, a blur,
the world's suddenness,
metal, air and a prayer
half-mouthed, spun,
flung into another plunge,
a curve swerving,
a tiny boat in a tempest—
and isn't this how we want
to live, live higher up,
hungry to leave the ground,
flinging sparks, the lights brighter,
the dark darker, bodies at war
with mere air, but still obedient
to the tracks laid down
to keep us on track.

Lesson with Flashcards

My daughter has leashed our dog to a doorknob
to teach him numbers
with flashcards—three sailboats on half the card,
the number 3 on the other. *Three*, she says,
so much love passing between them
I know I'm as close as I'll ever get
to how grass feels in the rain.

Bluebirds and wrens
dive hell-bent at the dogwood
for the last of the berries.
Hunger and love have the same stinging
insistence, but the berries will never last.

The itinerate handyman's just rattled up
through the pines, his wood-paneled Wagoneer
full of the bowels of furnaces, the bones
of appliances, hoses and ducts, every possible pipe—
his pulpit to all our falterings and dead stops.

I wave him on. Nothing needs fixing here.

Something Back to the Birds

To see what his father sees,
he stands on a chair
high enough for the same hammer-swing
at the birdhouse, to get every angle
merit-badge right, give something back
to the birds,
           the way he will shoot
the long snake, a bully
inching toward the bluebird eggs,
           then, that broken-winged thing
on his screened porch for weeks,
until at last he will hold the door open,
the bird's nerve up enough
for a take off.
           For now, though
on this chair, in the larger shadow
he will one day become, he's at work
nailing down the childhood he'll leave,
not wholly gone, but trailing
behind him
           like road dust.

Not Quite Ever After

Our kids, in the back of the bus,
are muttering, murdering
their own innocence—
                                    language
hurrying them headlong
toward an unblossoming.
Home from school they disappear
into a re-run's illusions—
                                    the flickering
less unbearable than the naked light bulb
in the long haul to the future.

The rest of us, still wearing
the heavy afternoon into evening
the floors still unswept,
watch commercials to remind us
what it was we used to want
someday.
                    No surprise we end up
unzipped in a hotel downtown
unsaying I love you, the marriage over
everyone always already knowing
the mistake it had been.

The East Berliner, 1989

They didn't come for the bananas,
but everyone who came through
that hole in the wall wanted one,
the West ready with its *Welkommen!*
mountains of yellow.
After twenty-eight years of concrete-cold
days and only those few flowers
defiant in the cracks of denial,
imagine the yellow-fresh sight,
that spike on the tongue,
the fireworks and flares
shot through the half-language
of heavy machines shattering
the cold Baltic chill, the half-song,
half-wail of horns, sirens and shouts
and behind it all, Beethoven's *9th*,
then that East Berliner, shuffling out,
hatless and dazed in a worm-eaten brown coat
to see it, and not believe it—
the bright yellow word he'll take home
to his wife, tight in his fist.

From the Chicago Train

in a square of dust behind a chain link fence
her thin, washed-to-death cotton print clings to her legs
an urgency in her far-off look
too tired to think all the way to words
and her child, three maybe, in coveralls
squat at some amusement with a stick
the sun a punishment
like the dirt brown sky

for just that long they are framed
in my train window, then gone

but it's Monday again, and that
was 30 years ago

if I could go back, I'd fill that porch
with flowers, loaves of bread and books
boxes and boxes of books
just to thank them

for lasting all these years
one more Madonna and child.

Abacus

Acela Express Claims Teenage Victims
—*The Trenton Times*

You don't need to know anything about trains
to know this one's hit something. You know

like you know someone's opened the front door
when you're upstairs in the shower, like you know,

even in your sleep, your husband's come to bed.
Your body gets its grip while gears and gaskets

wheeze and wheels skid to stop half-a-million tons
of train. You try to see through the thicket of deadly quiet,

mostly for what's nicking at the edges of other eyes
and mouths. You unfold the *New York Times*,

take out a pencil for the crossword, write "Elegy"
at 9 Across, sense the shuffling, the rising tension,

count how many letters in "Irreversible."
Lights go out, the air shuts down, cell phones emerge

for complaints about late arrivals: *Get someone else.*
Some kind of accident. No, I don't know what time.

Across the tracks a billboard with the mayor's picture
touts the city motto: Trenton Makes; the World Takes.

You sink into your seat like a sinner in too deep, try to think
of "Something You Can Still Count On" for 7 Down.

That First Leaving

Like a still life, all the silences within,
a mother and her fawn on the deck
stop munching the hostas to stare
eye-to-eye, watch me watch them

as if we are playing some child's game
and the loser moves first. No wonder
they are an easy mark. I want to warn them
there are people out there

but we've dragged ourselves out of sleep
for our son's early start, and still in our nightclothes
on the driveway, shift one foot to another at the edge
of thin air, the whole fabric of morning torn

and left behind: baseball cards, a mile of trains,
Matchbox cars, years of *National Geographic*
like parts of himself dropped off in stages
the rest piled in the car headed south
an arrow aimed beyond us

Violin

in ordinary wool on his way to work

      a meatloaf sandwich in his briefcase

he's back
      at her open window

            her song
a secret she can't keep
         slants and backtracks
a yellow kite riding orange air
          Boccherini
a luminescence
      breaking open
            the putty-colored day

it's intimate
      this listening
         this entering
someone else's dream
       the day widening

debris
    in a fist of wind
        blowing in from somewhere

Shambala

We are a circle being coached
in the art of meditation

            the idea
is a quiet mind, a calm abiding

            We have come
Jordan, Matt, Bruce, their PTSD and me
to practice, like a ballet class
how to hold a position
Buddha-like, each embracing
our own ruckus of aches and distractions
like scents luring a dog into the woods
my back with good intentions
and the lights overhead, a fluorescence
flickering toward dark

            On that floor
someone might have spent all day polishing
each of us is perched
a store of injustices and what-if's
hoping to discover a dignity deep as bones
legs sturdy enough for rough ground

                then somewhere a child
practices scales, that over-and-over
attempt at perfection

            Across town
the search for a body drags
into its ninth day in the weeds
and on that other coast
            the storm
the death toll still rising

From the Deck in Mid-November

The hydrangeas have one-by-one died from drowning or thirst
and, under so much growth overhead, less and less light every year

and the wild berries thinned, fewer birds. I miss the singing,
indoor songs, too—that safe way my sister and I had of testing

whether the house was too nervous for noise. We were just girls
when we screamed our names into a gorge, and unable to wait

for the echo, screamed again so our echoes and screams met
going and coming until the world filled up with our names.

Names hold sisters together like grass holds a hillside.
The older we get, the more we like hearing our names, but we wear them

now, she and I, like old women still wearing sweaters in the middle
of summer. A whole language is lost when no one is speaking its names.

A Substitute For Talking

Once you hear laughter and speak words
        bearing the weight of love or naked fear

you need that kind of sound. Creek-water
        patters at stones it pushes past

and without them has nothing to say
        so you add your own species of song.

It's a place you could listen all day.

Even after the boy leaves home, the ghost
        of him still speaks from behind his door

words that cloud and uncloud what you know
        about now, repeating the way

the sea curls and uncurls each
        glass-green wave, a churning sea foam

returning to your toes on the beach.

Discards

I'm culling the bookshelves for the yellowed
brittle to make room for new books.
That worn *Huck Finn* I taught for years
goes into the box, then I remember
how that inelegant boy could say the sun was sinking,
the Mississippi rising and make you smell
the swollen rot of the river; how he fried catfish
for whoever showed up to eat.
How those two strange shapes of grace,
outcast and fugitive, drifted half-naked and solemn,
nothing more than a fish hook on a piece of string.

I'd have thrown it out, too, that eyesore of a hammock
—dingy thing I once thought romantic between the birches—
except for the trouble of cutting it down, except
for our girl who loved it, throwing her arms up
on the upswing, giggling and reaching for the pull
she felt in the curve that wanted her back.

For the two of you

it comes down, at last, to this: the old dog
that settles on the bed between you

wanting his dull yellow coat stroked,
to the yellow on your hands, the color

of sunsets you once took the boat out to see,
the two closets of wooly sweaters, gray hairs

you'll brush off his shoulder before dinner,
his prescriptions, yours, test results

to the one thing we finally learn—the heat
of a hand, the amount of heart in a touch.

I don't know yet

  how it will feel
to wake up, sheets
on his side of the bed
unrumpled
the suddenness
of his fishing cap
on a nail in the shed
the worn spot on the bill
where his thumbprint
started and finished each trip

  how it will feel
to want the groan
of the floorboards
under his long steps
to sense him
in the room like air
pushed through a wind chime
and me looking back
at what I'll already know
won't be there

Connemara

The kiss of rain rinses the road
and even in all this hurt air,
the trees keep sending green, every
new leaf enough to keep us
watching for blossoms.

                       Then lightning
graffitis the bog's torn gray-rag sky,
an oarless boat's dead weight scars
the sand, unintention a hinge
that's pushed it in and back in, wind
that used to be breath
                       dead still now.

There's not enough light to call this
morning, but here's untouched time,
and the leaves will go on
pushing their way out of the pithy dark
to give us April,
a good place to lay down our grief.

Delta to West Palm

All pudge and dimples, the toddler
negotiates the empty chairs,
crossed feet and carry-ons at gate C-4
drops an orange into my lap.
"Here!" he says, then takes it back,
that "here" still behind his eyes
down the plane's aisle with his mom
to find their seats.

Once airborne, the tuxedoed thirty-something
next to me, (one empty seat between us)
settles into his earphones,
lowers his tray table and the one between us
to spread an oversized musical score
and unaware of me, cues first this, then that
musician in his mind—a symphony at 30,000 feet—
his hands in flight urging a music I can't hear,
a gift like the orange I didn't taste.

Three times in an hour, I am lifted.

NOTES

On Stone Mountain

The fairy shrimp, *Branchinella lithaca,* survives dry periods on Stone Mountain as a dormant, encapsulated embryo in temporary pools found in shallow rock depressions that periodically fill with rainwater. The pools also support other plants and animals, including two plants listed by the Federal and Georgia State governments, the black-spored quillwort and the little amphianthus. The fairy shrimp are not known to be found anywhere else.

The Fish Houses

Set on pilings in Pine Island Sound and Charlotte Harbor, the fish houses, a string of shacks, built by the fishing industry as ice houses, net mending stations or just shanties where the fishermen bunked out on the water without electricity, plumbing or telephones, are still standing nearly 90 years later.

On the National Register of Historic places, they are the legacy of the thriving industry that worked the waters before World War II. Fishermen stored their catch in the fish companies' ice houses where boats picked up the harvest and carried it to Punta Gorda.

"When the heart dies, it dies entire"

A line from Kurt Brown's poem "Massive," in *More Things in Heaven and Earth* (Four Way Books, 2002)

Mars, a Mike de Kock-trained four-year-old, Irish bred by Galileo out of Massarra, veered away from the field uncontrollably after two furlongs at the Sheema Classic in Dubai, March 29, 2014 and "went down in a scramble of legs" at the far rail when he suffered a massive cardiac event. Irish Jockey, Richard Hughes, thrown into bushes over the rail at Mars' collapse, sustained a fractured vertebra but was not seriously hurt.

The Honor System

One of the major western tributaries of the Mississippi River, the Arkansas river (pronounced ar KAN zes in Kansas and Colorado and AR kan saw in Arkansas) meanders 1,450 miles across four states from its mouth where it springs forth in the Colorado Rocky Mountains, about 10 miles north of Leadville, Colorado. From there it flows through the Royal Gorge, then east into the Midwest via Kansas, and finally into the South through Oklahoma and Arkansas where it meets up with the Mississippi in Desha County, just north of Arkansas City. Since 1902, Kansas has claimed Colorado takes too much of the river's water, resulting in legal disputes even to this day. Further, the river has fallen victim to years of groundwater irrigation that has sucked dry the basin that scientists say took 60 million years to form, the aquifer dropping an average of 1 1/2 feet per year since 1966. With evaporation, percolation and miles of irrigation ditches diverting water to crops along its route, water released upstream often fails to survive the two-day trip to Kansas. Scientists expect the underground water supply to be completely exhausted by 2050 at which time the Arkansas will be a dead river.

Whitman's Hermit Thrush

The hermit thrush is the bird in Walt Whitman's "When Lilacs Last in the Dooryard Bloom'd," an elegy on the death of Abraham Lincoln.

> Solitary the thrush,
> The hermit withdrawn to himself, avoiding the settlements,
> Sings by himself a song.

Asylum

The Willard State Hospital for the Chronic Insane officially opened in New York October 13, 1869 to receive its first patient, Mary Rote, who, chained at the wrists, was transported by steamboat from the Columbia County Poorhouse. At its peak, it housed more than 4,000 "inmates." With the average stay being 30 years, most never left." and over 5,800 are buried in numbered graves in the hospital cemetery. Sometime after its closing in 1995, more than 400 suitcases were found, containing the personal belongings the inmates brought with them, suitcases that were never opened or passed on to survivors.

The Willard story is told in *The Lives They Left Behind: Suitcases from a State Hospital Attic*, by Darby Penney, Peter Shastny with Lisa Rinzler, photographer (Bellevue Literary Press, Reprint Edition, 2009).

At the Holy Well of Tobernalt

Tobernalt at Sligo, originally *Tober ne nAlt*, an Anglicization of the Irish phrase that roughly means "well in the cliff," is a natural spring well that established itself in a primeval forest and has been flowing continuously for over 6,000 years, predating Ireland's Celtic ancestors who gathered there to celebrate the festival of Lughanasa, their harvest festival, now known as Garland Sunday, where the faithful still walk in pilgrimage to Tobernalt from Sligo for the first Mass at 6am.

Christianized by St. Patrick, Tobernalt provided one of the "Mass rocks" where Priests said Mass during Penal times in Ireland, the period where English law controlled the religious rights of the Catholic population and the celebration of the Mass was prohibited. People flocked to Tobernalt when news spread by word of mouth that the priest, who traveled in disguise with a price on his head, was expected. The faithful set out the night before to journey in small quiet groups to be at Tobernalt before dawn. A close watch was kept against surprise attack by soldiers.

Gravity

Born in 1838, Annie Edson, at seventeen, from a substantial family, says, in her autobiographical account, that she married S. David Taylor, a marriage that was never substantiated, since there is no record of their marriage and no genealogical record of an S. David Taylor. Her story that he was killed in the Civil War has also proven to be untrue by virtue of the dates she offers. A woman with a heightened personal sense of dignity, Annie Taylor taught piano, manners, dance and, finally, acrobatics when, at the turn of the century, "no one wanted waltzes" and "no one set a value on civility" and her hundred students had dwindled to only a few. With her "rent overdue," "a tab run-up for food" and "winter coming on with a need for new boots," she made her desperate plan to be the first to take the leap over Niagara Falls for the wealth she expected from notoriety.

On October 24th, her 63rd birthday (though she professed to be only 43), one and one-half miles above the brink of the Horseshoe

Falls, Annie Edson Taylor climbed inside the barrel she'd designed and had built to her own specifications. With the barrel's lid in place, 100 pounds of air bicycle-pumped inside, the men in the boat pulling the barrel along cut the rope to set her loose on the 20-minute trip over the 158 ft. drop of Horseshoe Falls.

Though she survived, she quickly and sadly realized the observers would have liked the story better if she had died. Expecting a daredevil, young and muscled, to emerge from the barrel, observers were disappointed at the battered wreck of a woman who climbed out and, instead of being heralded as she'd hoped, she was derided. "It's Methuselah's wife," one jeered. "If they had left it up to me," another crowed, "I'd have left her in the barrel," and the crowds that had come to see her as "a sideshow attraction" moved on with "hoots and catcalls" to see the "Naughty Spanish Dancer" and the "bloody spot outside the Temple of Music where McKinley had been shot the month before."

Annie Edson Taylor spent the next few years traveling with her barrel, posing for photographs in small-town store windows and signing post cards for pennies, until her barrel was stolen, and the crowds dwindled from fifty to ten, then three, then none, and she found herself buried under bills for hotels and meals, trains and carriages and gratuities for river men, physicians, the police and reporters, her chiseling manager, the drunken Frank Russell, having gone north with her barrel to create his own more exciting sideshow, himself the hero. As a final insult, she was asked to sign a release for her story for a play where "an actress, young and beautiful," would play Annie, a "pleading heroine," set adrift by a "villainous husband." Her rescuer, a handsome sailor, would be played, of course, by Frank Russell. After even more set-backs, disappointments and disillusionments, she gave up trying to earn acknowledgment for her stunt:

> I had tried ten thousand times to tell the world where I had gone.
>
> But I never found the words to match its force
>
> Now I felt most true to it—
>
> when I was able to keep still.

At 82, she died a ward of the charity she'd struggled all her life to avoid.

Murray, Joan. *Queen of the Mist*, (Boston, Beacon Press, 1999).

The East Berliner, 1989

In a single day, roads blocked off for nearly 30 years were open to traffic, and "people in Hamburg and other West German cities along the East German border awoke to find convoys of drably dressed people driving dilapidated East German cars through their streets in search of—of all things—bananas," that delicacy no East Berliner had seen since the wall went up in 1961.

"When Bananas Brought Down the Berlin Wall," *Zee News*, November 8, 2009.

In Gratitude

for Thomas Lux for his extraordinary friendship, encouragement and generous spirit

for Tom Lombardo for seeing into the heart of these poems and for selecting and shaping the manuscript with his sharp editor's eye

for Press 53's Kevin Morgan Watson for shaping these pages into a book and for his respect for the work

for the entire faculty of the Warren Wilson MFA Program in Poetry, especially Ellen Bryant Voigt, Jennifer Grotz, David Baker, the late Steve Orlen, Martha Rhodes and Eleanor Wilner for their enormous contributions in sharpening my craft and guiding these poems from their earliest drafts

for Rebecca Foust for her faith in my work and for staying close with her generous support and encouragement

for the poetry communities of Poetry at Tech, Sarah Lawrence Summer Seminars, the Palm Beach Poetry Festival, The Frost Place, the Iowa Summer Writers' Workshop and the countless workshop leaders and participants who read these poems in all stages of their development and encouraged them forward

for the love and friendship of Laure-Anne Bosselaar and the late Kurt Brown

for my sister, Veleda, who, with me, shows up in the "we" in many of these poems, who was proud of this work and someone I miss every day

for my husband, Clyde Mynatt, who generously made room for poetry in my life and wholeheartedly supports me every possible way

for all the people who appear in these poems, especially my two children, Arienne and Jason, both of whom shine in these poems as they do in my life

GINGER MURCHISON started writing poetry after a thirty-one-year teaching career. She earned her MFA from Warren Wilson College. Together with Thomas Lux, she helped found POETRY at TECH, at the Georgia Institute of Technology,where she served as associate director for five years and as one of its Visiting McEver Chairs in Poetry. She serves as a member of the Board of Trustees of The Frost Place, is a member of the conference faculty for the Palm Beach Poetry Festival, and is Editor in Chief of the acclaimed *Cortland Review*. She has two grown children, Arienne and Jason, and lives with her husband Clyde Mynatt in Ft. Myers, Florida.

Cover artist DAWN D. SURRATT studied art at the University of North Carolina at Greensboro as a recipient of the Spencer Love Scholarship in Fine Art. She has exhibited her work throughout the southeast and currently works as a freelance designer and artist. Her work has been published internationally in magazines, on book covers, and in print media. She lives on the beautiful Kerr Lake in northern North Carolina with her husband, one demanding cat and a crazy Pembroke Welsh Corgi.